Shape-a-Story

Reproducible Story Shapes and Ideas for Creative Writing Booklets

by Janice L. Auld

Fearon Teacher Aids
Carthage, Illinois

Designer: Diane Hoyt-Goldsmith
Illustrator: Heidi Chang

ISBN-0-8224-6392-X

Printed in the United States of America

1. 9 8 7 6

Contents

Introduction

Shape-a-Story is designed to help you add excitement to creative writing assignments. Attractively illustrated covers to cut and color, together with seasonal themes and a variety of story-starter ideas, add up to a motivating mixture for your creative writing program.

Shape-a-Story writing projects may be used for both primary and elementary grades, as well as in many special education classes. In addition to their use in creative writing projects, the shapes may be used to provide incentive for writing reports in other subject areas.

For each writing project, reproduce the cover art and as many writing pages as needed. You may wish to provide additional pages if your students will be doing rough drafts. Use the suggestions on the teacher's page to stimulate discussion and get students started. Have your students cut and color the covers, adding their story titles and "by-lines." Staple the completed writing pages to the covers. Or, instead of having students create individual booklets, you may want to create a class book with each student contributing a page.

The teacher's page for each project provides not only suggestions for story starters, but also a word list that you may want to offer students and additional activities for other subject areas. A fully illustrated bulletin board with directions for construction gives you an attractive way to display your students' work.

When you are teaching creative writing, it is important to remember that creativity is not a subject, but a process. Your students' stories may need to go through several drafts. Some children may have a burst of creative energy, while others may need more time for quiet thought. The ideas presented here are only another set of tools to be used for teaching creative writing. You should provide motivation from a variety of sources, such as songs, stories, poems, and pictures. Creativity can be sparked, kindled, and allowed to grow when there is stimulation, motivation, and encouragement of the process as well as praise for the product.

Traveling Train

Story Starters

1. You may wish to read a story, suited to your students' abilities, with a train theme or element. Topics for discussion might include how railroad tracks are laid, the kinds of cargo trains carry, different kinds of engines, and the design of passenger cars.
2. To stimulate students' imaginations, ask them to close their eyes and imagine they are seated in green leather seats on a passenger train. Describe the sounds they might hear, such as the hiss of steam, the clickety-clack of the wheels, the toot of the whistle. Tell them that suddenly a long boa constrictor enters their compartment, coils up on a seat, doffs a red cap, and says . . . Ask the students to finish the story for their booklets.
3. These story-starter phrases may be printed on the writing sheet master before duplicating, or they may be dictated to students.

A tiger jumped off the train . . .	Once I rode in a boxcar . . .
A small engine left the track . . .	On a train, I met . . .

Vocabulary Development

caboose	boxcar	conductor	passenger	railroad
whistle	engineer	tracks	tickets	trestle

Additional Activity: Social Studies

Use the train booklets in a social studies transportation unit. Students may write about train travel in the present and the past, types of cargo, or the kinds of engines used to pull trains.

Bulletin Board Ideas

With a black marker, draw a track on the background paper. Pin the completed engine booklets on the track. Prepare a caption and pin it to the board. Cut puffs of smoke from white paper and on them print new vocabulary words or words relating to the theme of the bulletin board. Pin the puffs above the engines as shown in the illustration. Add appropriate background elements.

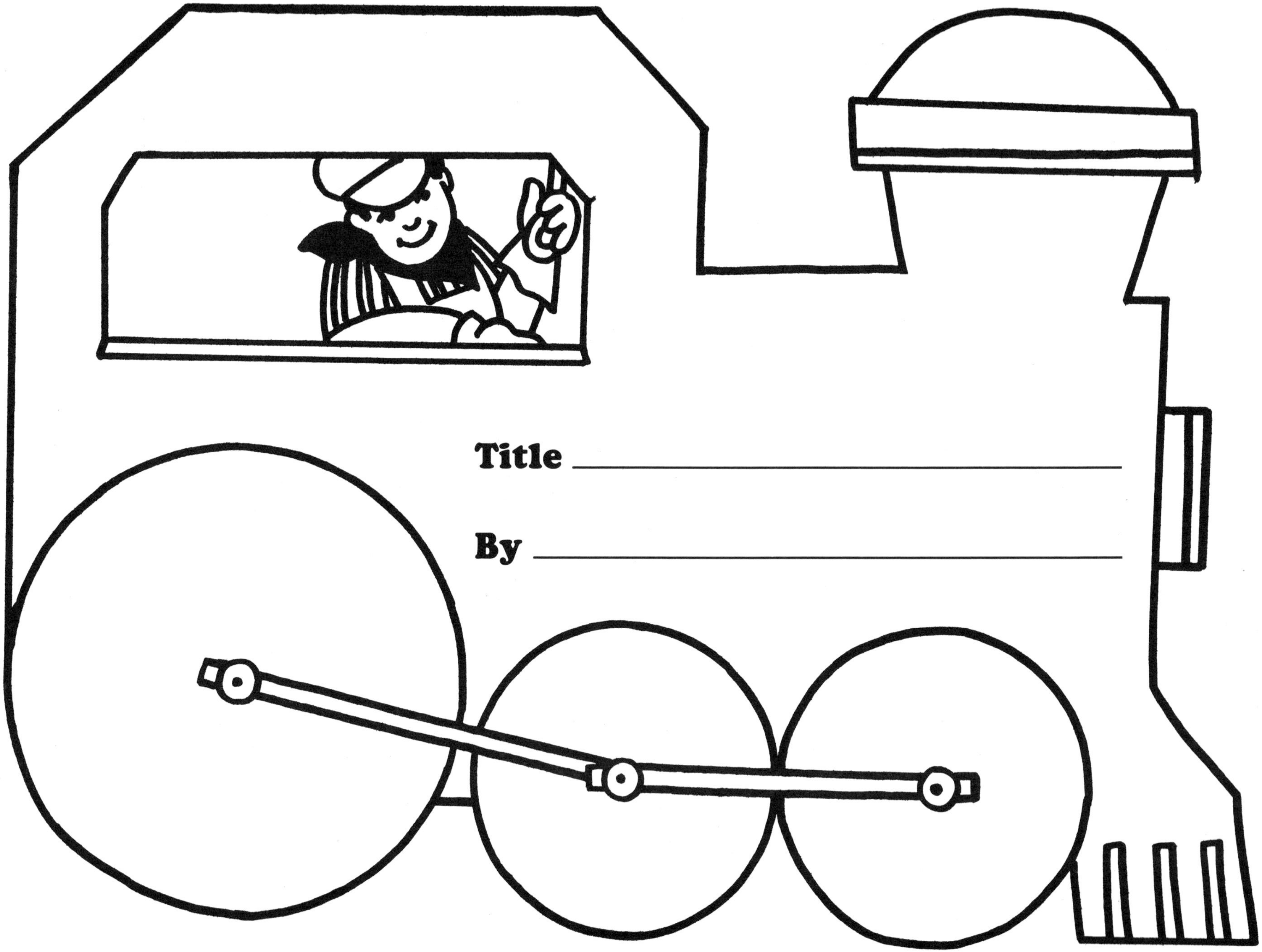
Title ______________________
By ______________________

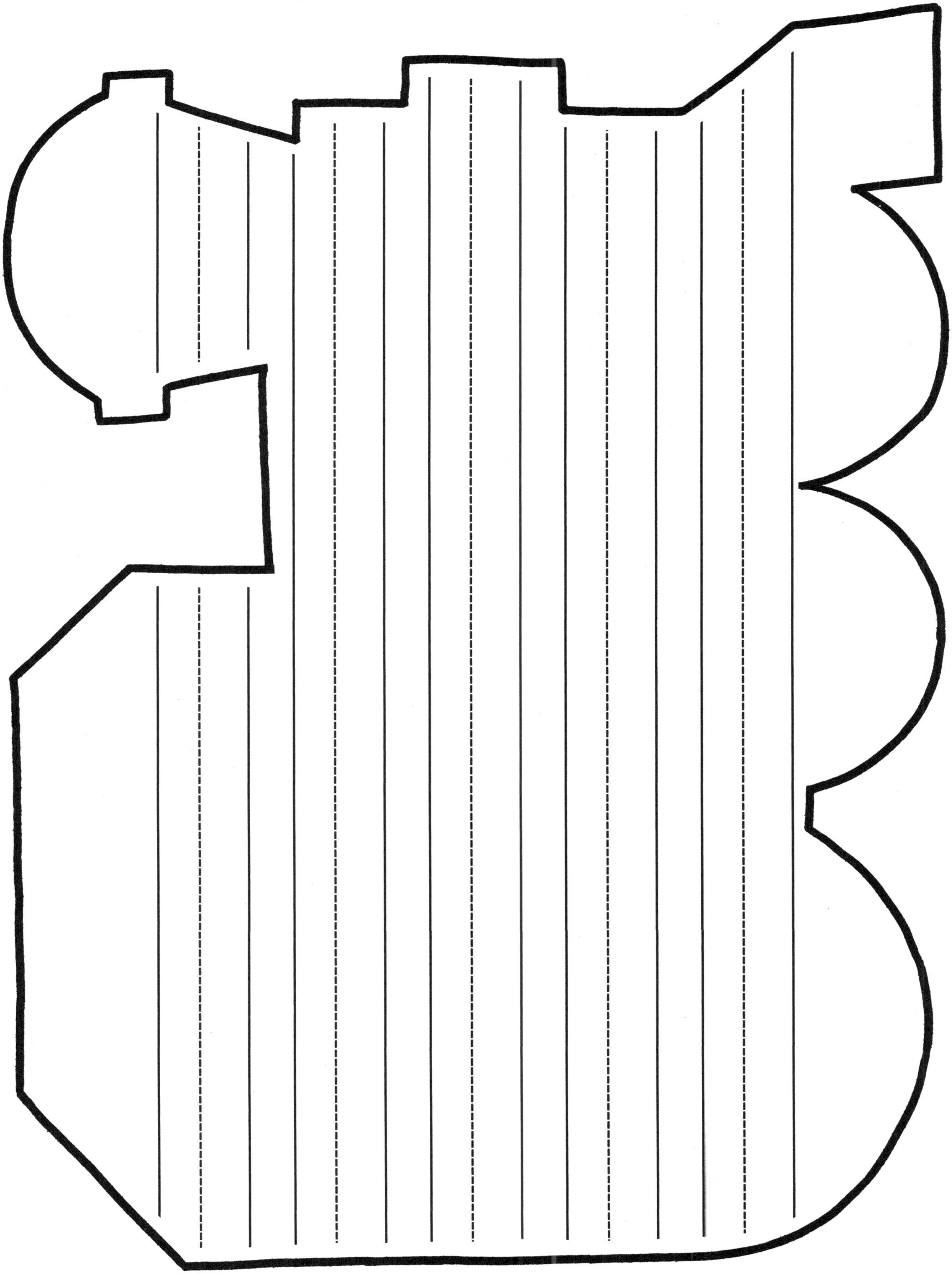

Sail Away!

Story Starters

1. You may want to introduce this project with a seafaring folk song or a short story with a sailboat element. Topics for discussion might include how boats are made and the materials that are used for making them, sails and wind, and how sailboats are controlled by the tiller. Students may be able to share sailing experiences.
2. To stimulate students' imaginations, ask them to plan trips on sailboats. Tell them to describe the sizes of the boats, the number of friends who will go along, the places they'll drop anchor, and the kinds of foods they will take along. Ask them to write about what happens on their boats when a big tuna jumps on board and . . .
3. These story-starter phrases may be printed on the writing sheet master before duplicating, or they may be dictated to students.

Once, I built a sailboat . . .	The captain of the boat . . .
My sailboat sprang a leak . . .	When I was a sailor, I . . .

Vocabulary Development

sail	ocean	sea	anchor	mast	dock
lake	sailor	waves	tide	deck	harbor

Additional Activity: Science

Let students construct sailboats using walnut shell halves. They will each need a walnut half; a toothpick for a mast; two small paper triangles, pasted together with the top of the toothpick between them; and a marble-sized bit of modeling clay to hold the mast in the walnut. Supervise while the students experiment with a tub of water, the walnut sailboats, and various wind sources such as a bellows, a folded paper, or an electric fan. Students may record their observations in the sailboat booklets.

Bulletin Board Ideas

Pin the sailboat booklets on a blue background. Use dark blue or black marker to draw ripples in the water. Cut lily pads from green construction paper and print vocabulary words on them. Create a shoreline with green paper and flowers. Print the caption on white paper clouds.

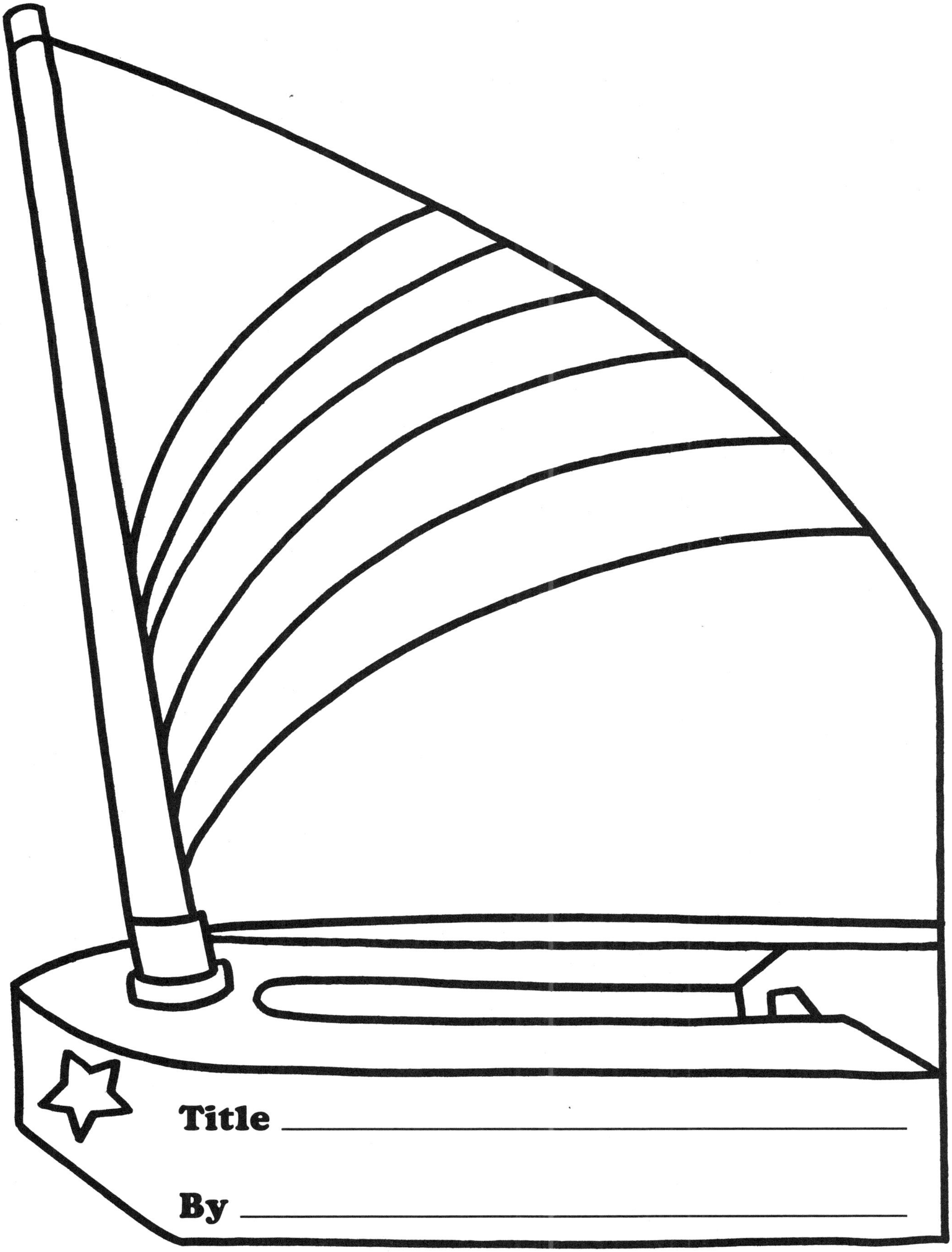
Title
By

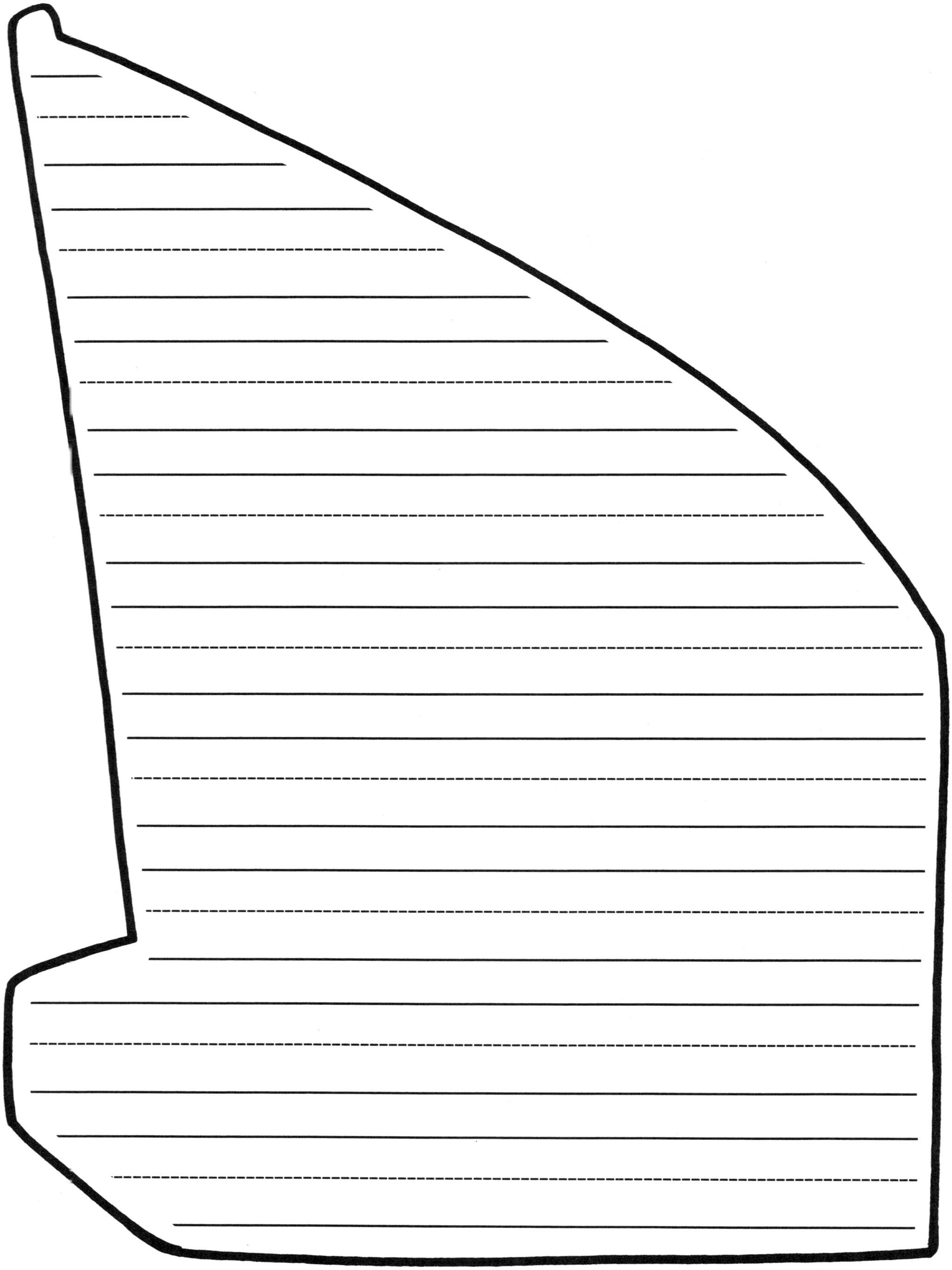

Literate Leaves

Story Starters

1. In the fall, you may wish to discuss falling leaves and take a nature walk to admire fall colors. In the spring, you could ask students to notice new leaves and varying shades of green. Topics for discussion might include leaves and the seasons, varieties of trees, and leaf forms.
2. To stimulate students' creativity, ask them each to imagine living in a tree house high in the branches of a strong old tree. Tell them to write about their tree houses. Ask each of them to describe what happens when a family of squirrels builds a nest in the tree house.
3. These story-starter phrases may be printed on the writing page master before duplicating, or they may be dictated to students.

   The little yellow leaf fell . . . I found a magic leaf that . . .

   When it rained, the leaves . . . Living on the leaf there was a . . .

Vocabulary Development

autumn	season	rake	spring	vein	oak
fall	crisp	tree house	stem	birch	maple

Additional Activity: Art

Have students collect leaves and bark and use crayons to make rubbings on unlined leaf-shaped paper. Ask them to label the leaves and bark with the names of the trees they came from. After students cut out their leaf shapes, have a "leafy" art exhibit or display the rubbings on a bulletin board.

Bulletin Board Ideas

Make a tree trunk and branches from brown or black corrugated paper. Pin the tree to a board covered with blue paper. Attach the leaf booklets to the tree branches and scatter a few on the ground under the tree. You may wish to add some leaves collected on a nature walk, or use paper leaves that have vocabulary words printed on them. Prepare a caption for the board as shown in the illustration.

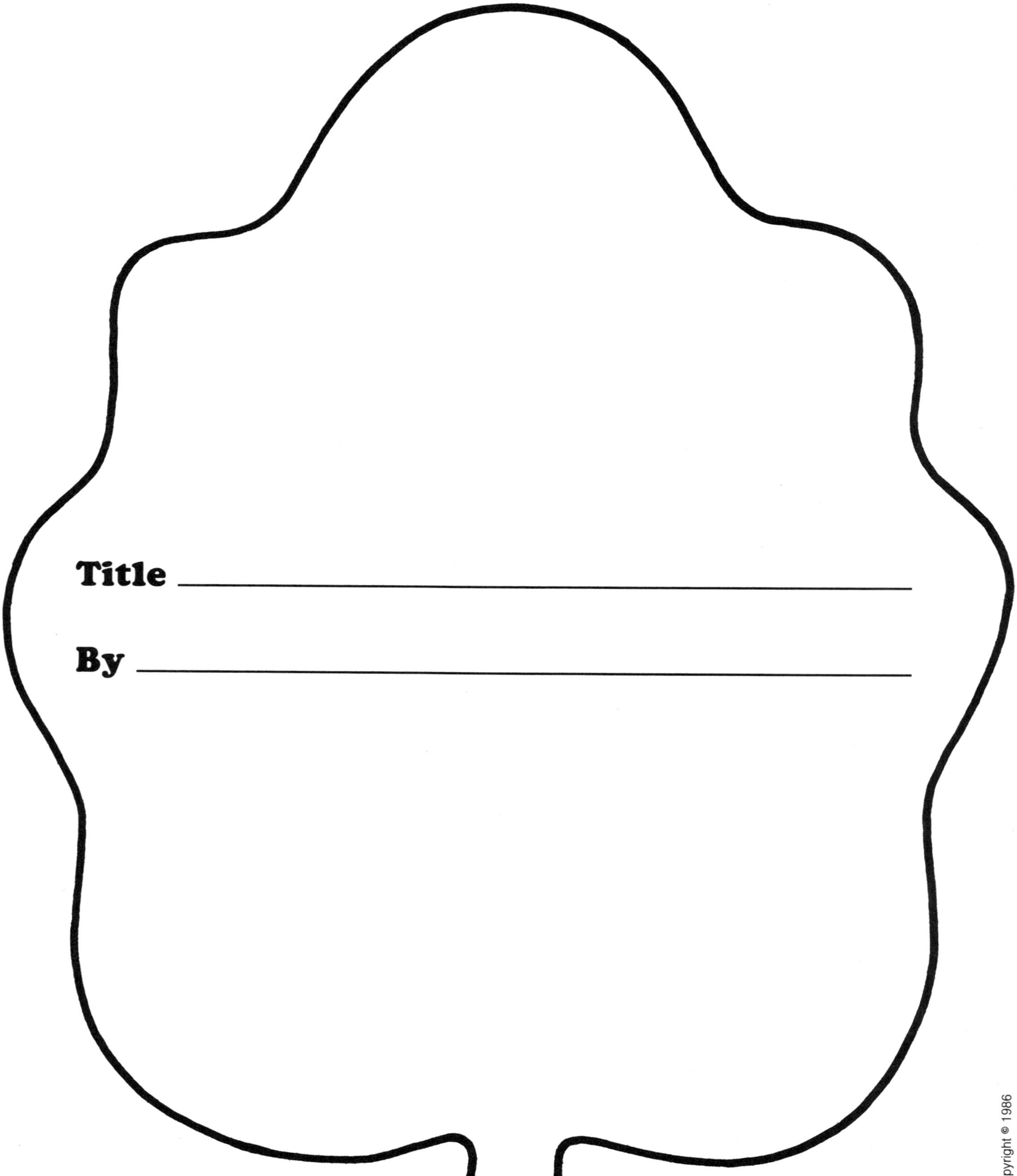
Title ______________________________
By ______________________________

Pumpkin Patch Prose

Story Starters

1. You may wish to bring a pumpkin to class and carve a jack-o'-lantern face while students observe. Read a Halloween story or poem for the class.
2. To stimulate imaginations, tell the students they should visualize Halloween night and the dark sky. All the houses on all the streets are dark, except for the candles flickering in jack-o'-lanterns. Ask them each to imagine walking along with friends, wearing costumes and carrying trick-or-treat bags, when suddenly the wind begins to blow, and a jack-o'-lantern says . . . Ask the students each to write what the jack-o'-lantern said.
3. These story-starter phrases may be printed on the writing sheet master before duplicating, or they may be dictated to students.

On Halloween, I saw . . .	A big pumpkin rolled . . .
My costume is . . .	A black cat ran . . .

Vocabulary Development

pumpkin	jack-o'-lantern	Halloween	costume	witch
patch	carve	ghost	goblin	bats

Additional Activity: Language Arts

Have students write descriptive phrases or words for Halloween. Give them some examples: words such as *fun, costumes, scary;* and phrases —Halloween is dark; trick or treat. Let students illustrate the words and phrases with drawings or cut-out pictures. Display the booklets for Halloween.

Bulletin Board Ideas

Use twisted green craft paper or heavy green yarn for vines. Pin the completed pumpkin booklets on the vines and add construction paper leaves that have vocabulary words printed on them. Prepare a caption and pin it to the bulletin board.

Title ______________________________

By ______________________________

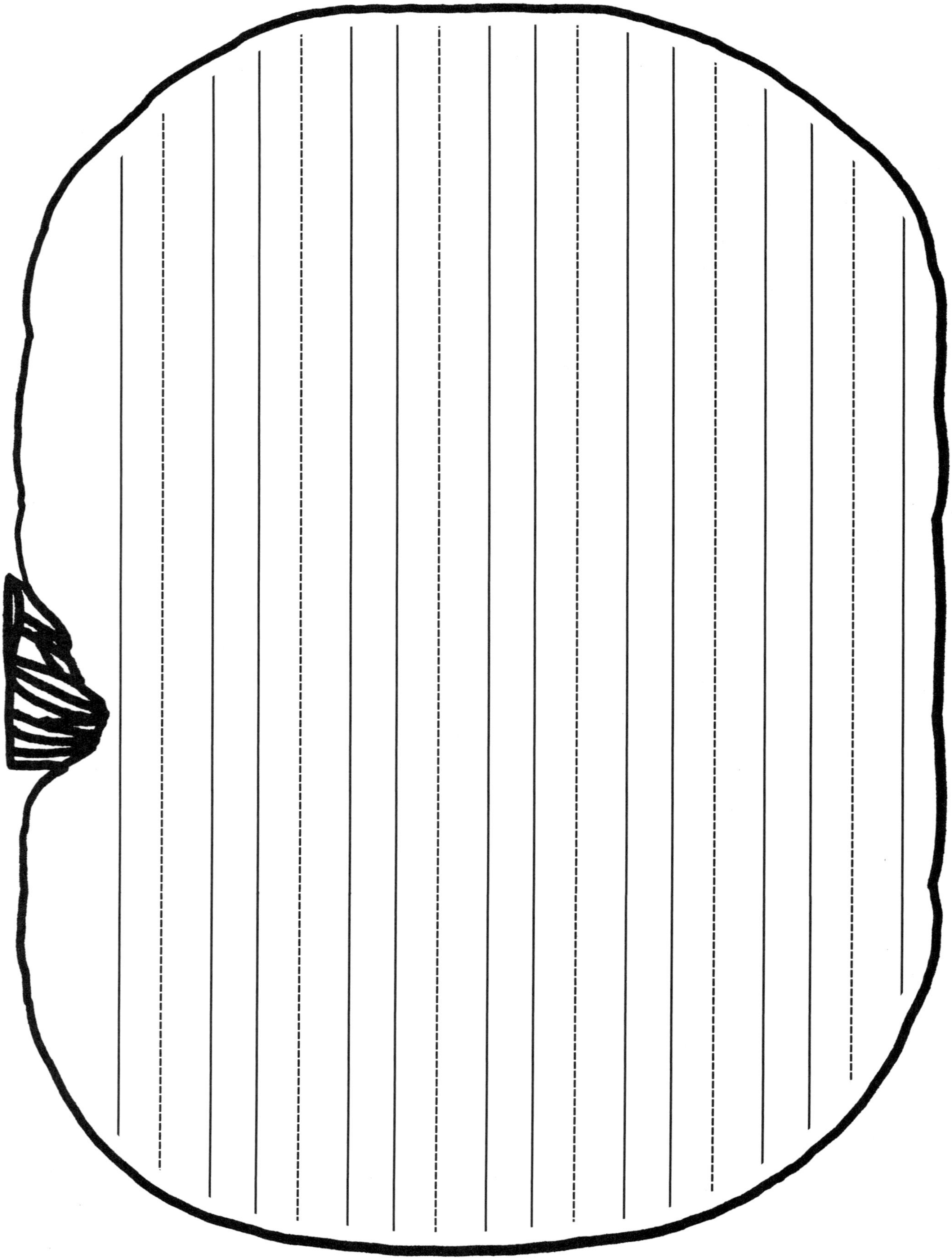

Story Pies

Story Starters

1. Discuss the preparation of pies with the students. Describe how a filling is placed between two crusts. Ask the students about their favorite pies and list them on the chalkboard. You may wish to introduce rhymes such as "Sing a Song of Sixpence" or "Little Jack Horner" into the discussion.
2. To stimulate imaginations, ask the students to think about the first Thanksgiving and a long table covered with many kinds of foods, including pies. Tell the students to write about what they would choose to eat from the imaginary table and to describe their Thanksgiving feasts.
3. These story-starter sentences are like pie crusts—a top sentence and a bottom sentence. Ask your students to add the filling! You may print the top sentence on the first lines of the writing sheet master and the bottom sentence at the bottom of the sheet before duplicating, or write the sentences on the chalkboard.

Top Sentence	**Bottom Sentence**
That is my pie!	I will never eat that again.
Once, I made a pie.	The last dish was washed.
A small mouse saw the pie.	The two mice fell asleep.

Vocabulary Development

crust	pumpkin	bake	oven	flour	rolling pin
filling	apple	cherry	flaky	stove	apron

Additional Activity: Cooking

Let students participate in the preparation of a class pie using no-bake crusts and instant pie filling.

Bulletin Board Ideas

Pin pie booklets on the board to make a bakery scene. You or the students can make baker figures from tagboard. Hinge the arm joints with brass fasteners. Dress the figures with scraps of cloth or crepe paper. Use yarn for hair. Print new vocabulary words on paper cutouts of bowls and spoons. Prepare a caption and pin it to the board.

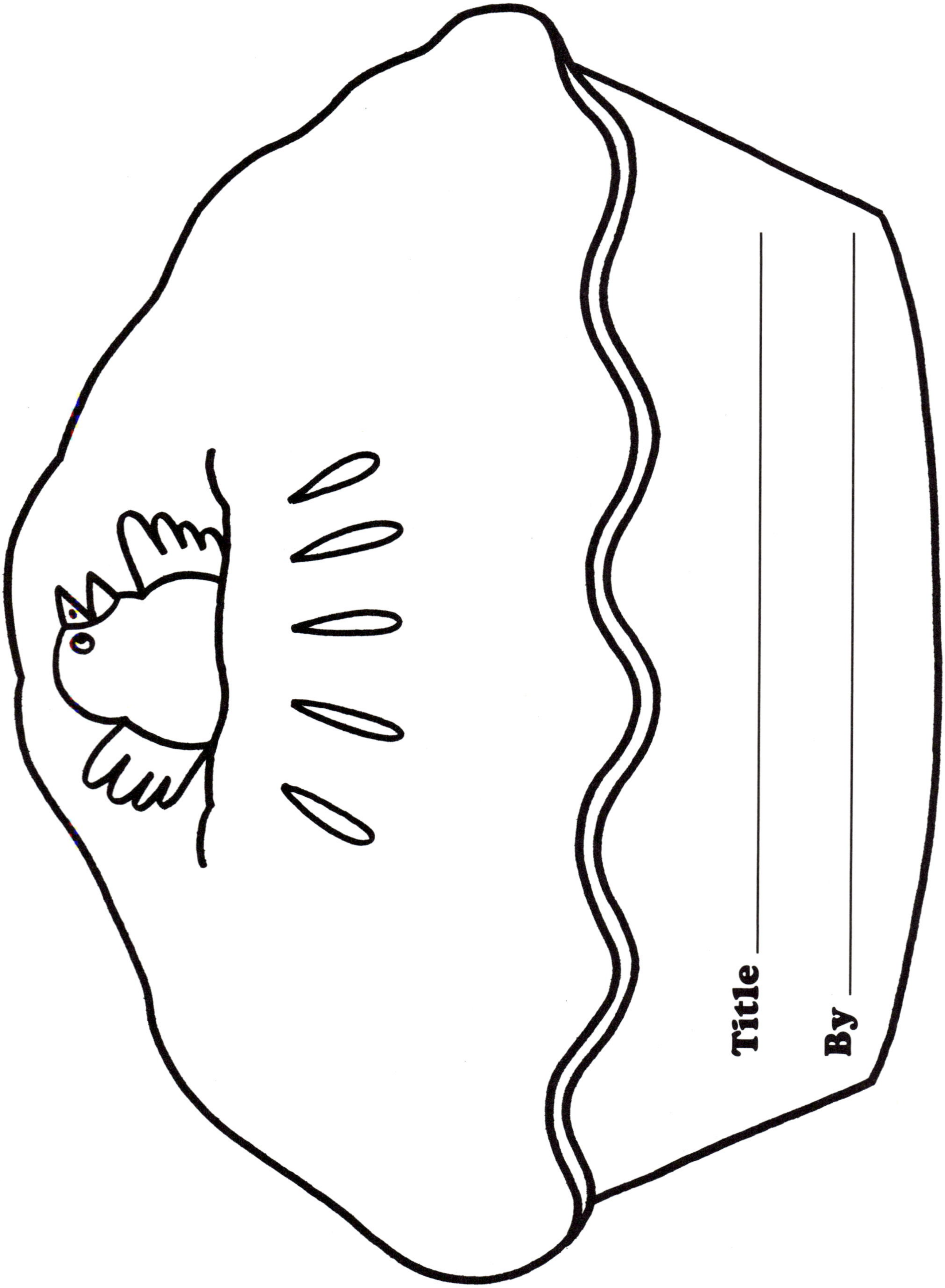
Title
By

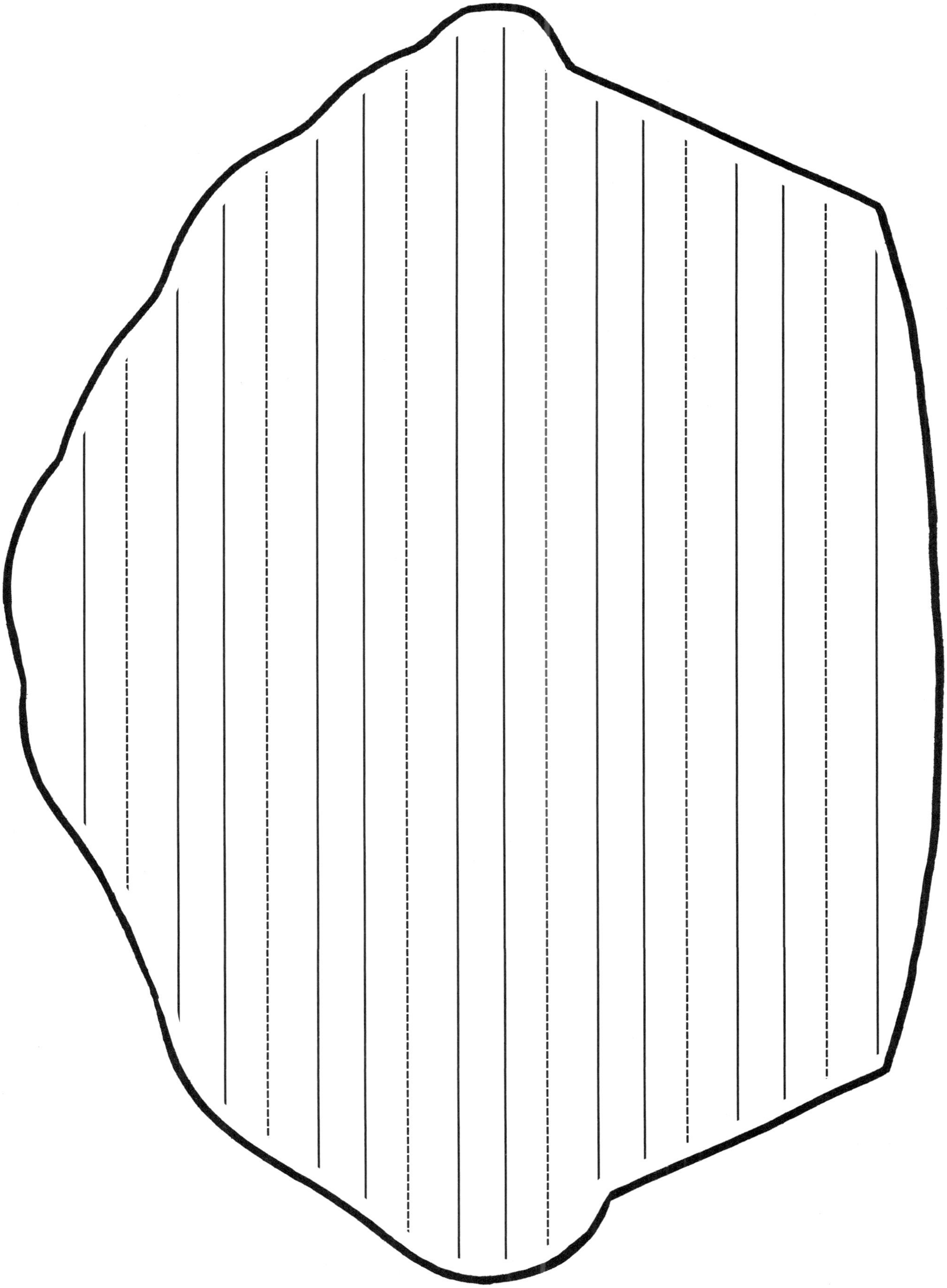

Apple Story Orchard

Story Starters

1. You may want to share the story of Johnny Appleseed with your students, or read them the story of William Tell. Topics for discussion could include varieties of apples, how they grow, and the many uses of apples.
2. To stimulate imaginations, ask the students to pretend they have each been stranded on an uninhabited island in the middle of a wide river. The only food on the island comes from an apple tree full of delicious apples. This apple tree is the only tree on the island. Ask the students to write about how they live on the island and how they manage to get off the island and back to their homes.
3. These story-starter phrases may be printed on the writing sheet master before duplicating, or they may be dictated to the students.

   Once I planted an apple seed . . .   There is a worm in my apple . . .

   Our apple tree is . . .   An apple fell off the tree . . .

Vocabulary Development

applesauce	core	cider	fruit	ripe	juicy
orchard	slice	vinegar	bushel	tart	sweet

Additional Activity: Art

Bring a supply of apples to class and cut them in halves. Provide each student with half an apple, several colors of liquid tempera, and a brush. Ask the students to paint the apple halves with tempera and make prints on the cut-out apple-shape covers. They should use several colors for their prints. Use the decorated covers with the story pages and display the students' work.

Bulletin Board Ideas

Twist brown craft paper to make a large tree trunk and branches. Make leaves from green paper and print new vocabulary words on them. Hang apple booklets and leaves from the branches. Scatter a few booklets and leaves on the ground under the tree. Prepare a caption and pin it to the board.

Holiday Trees

Story Starters

1. You may want to teach your students the song "Oh, Tannenbaum" in German. Or read a story with an evergreen tree in it. Topics for discussion could include the meaning of *evergreen,* the shape of evergreen leaves (needles), and uses of evergreen trees and boughs for holiday decorations.
2. To stimulate imaginations, bring some pine boughs into the class. The fragrance of the boughs should be noted as you tell the students to imagine they are walking through a pine forest. There is snow on the ground, and the wind is very still. Ask them each to write about what happens when a dark shadow crosses the path in the imaginary forest.
3. These story-starter phrases may be printed on the writing sheet master before duplicating, or they may be dictated to students.

My holiday tree is . . .	Under the tree, I found . . .
On my tree, I put . . .	The sad little tree . . .

Vocabulary Development

evergreen	boughs	trim	fir	forest
needles	wreath	pine	decorate	woods

Additional Activity: Science

Have students research evergreen trees and write about each species they read about. Students can illustrate the needles of each species, such as pine (several varieties), fir, spruce, and redwood.

Bulletin Board Ideas

Pin the completed tree booklets on a white background to make a holiday tree forest. Print new vocabulary words on small green tree cutouts and add the cutouts to the scene. Use black yarn to make hills and valleys. Prepare a caption and pin it to the board.

Title ____________________
By ____________________

A Winter's Tale

Story Starters

1. You may wish to read seasonal stories or teach your students some old-time songs such as "Frosty." Topics for discussion could include seasonal changes in the weather and favorite winter activities—such as skiing, ice skating, and sledding.
2. To stimulate students' imaginations, ask them each to picture a hill covered with snow. Tell them they are standing at the top of the hill with a small snowball. Ask them to pretend to throw the snowball so high up in the air that it disappears, only to return carrying a . . . Tell the students each to write about what the snowball brought back.
3. These story-starter phrases may be printed on the writing sheet master before duplicating, or they may be dictated to the students.

   The snowman told Mr. Sun . . . The snowman was sad . . .

   A snowman came into the house . . . I made a big snowman . . .

Vocabulary Development

snowball	ice	melt	white	mittens
snowflake	winter	icicle	frozen	boots

Additional Activity: Art

Provide students with white paper and scissors. Help them cut several styles of snowflakes. Use the snowflakes to add decorative touches to the bulletin board.

Bulletin Board Ideas

Cover a bulletin board with blue background paper. Use cotton batting or fiberfill to make a field of snow. Pin the completed snowman booklets to the board. Cut green trees, write vocabulary words on them, and pin them to the board. Use students' snowflakes for added decoration. Prepare a caption and pin it to the board.

Title ________________________________

By ________________________________

Sweet Fantasies

Story Starters

1. You may wish to play part of the *Nutcracker Suite,* especially "The Dance of the Sugar Plum Fairy," for the students. Topics for discussion could include how hard candies are made, and how candy canes were used to decorate trees in the past.
2. To stimulate students' imaginations, saturate small strips of paper with peppermint flavoring and distribute them to the children. Ask the children to smell the peppermint-scented strips—why is it called *pepper*mint? Then have them picture a big pile of candy canes. Tell the students to write about what happens when one of the candy canes begins to grow taller and taller all by itself and suddenly . . . Ask the children to finish the tale.
3. These story-starter phrases may be printed on the writing sheet master before duplicating, or they may be dictated to the students.

A magic candy cane . . .	A silly candy cane said . . .
I ate so many sweet . . .	Once, a candy cane ran . . .

Vocabulary Development

peppermint	flavor	sweet	mint
stripes	holiday	candy cane	lollipop

Additional Activity: Social Studies

Have students research Christmas holiday celebrations in another country, such as Mexico. They can write about foods, observances, and customs.

Bulletin Board Ideas

Cover the board with red paper. Cut white clouds from construction paper and pin them to the board. Pin the completed candy cane booklets inside the clouds and add holly leaves with vocabulary words written on them. Prepare a caption and pin it to the board.

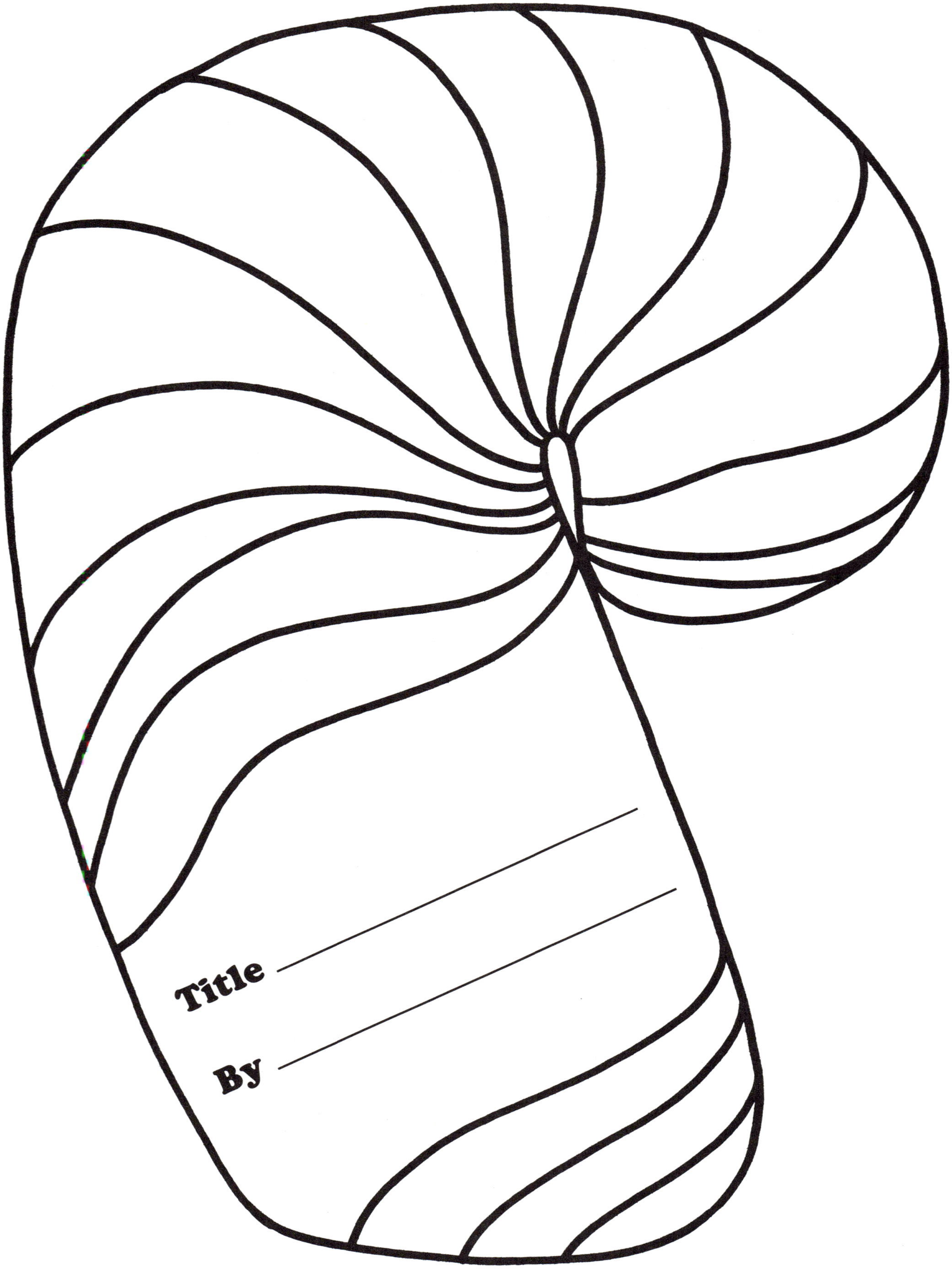
Title
By

Butterflies in Springtime

Story Starters

1. You may want to read a story or poem with a butterfly theme. Prints or books about butterflies are readily available and may interest students. Topics for discussion could include the development of a butterfly, its life span, and the difference between a butterfly and a moth.
2. To stimulate imaginations, ask the students to pretend they are all members of a butterfly family. It is time to move to another area, so they must all fly away. Ask each student to write about what happens when he or she is separated from the family and stops to rest for the night in a beautiful red pepper tree.
3. These story-starter phrases may be printed on the writing sheet master before duplicating, or they may be dictated to the students.

   A butterfly landed on my head . . .   Once, a butterfly said . . .

   The lost butterfly . . .   A sleepy butterfly . . .

Vocabulary Development

butterfly	cocoon	wings	moth
insect	hatch	caterpillar	antennae

Additional Activity: Art

Provide yarn, fabric, sequins, and glitter, and help students decorate their booklet covers.

Bulletin Board Ideas

On a blue background, pin the completed butterfly booklets to look as if they are hovering over a field of flowers. Make smaller butterflies and the flowers out of construction paper. Put vocabulary words on the small butterflies. Prepare a caption and pin it to the board.

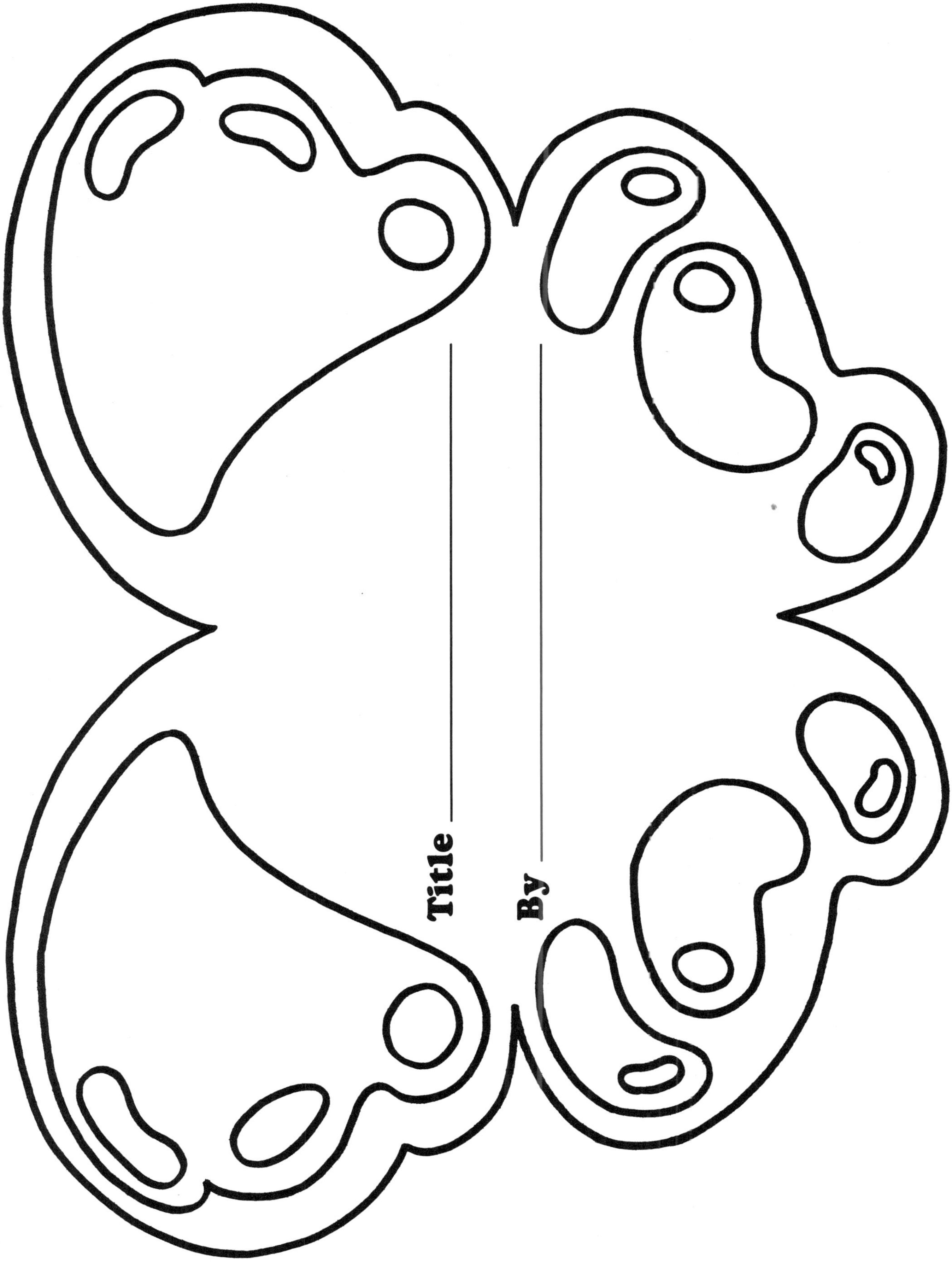
Title ______________________
By ______________________

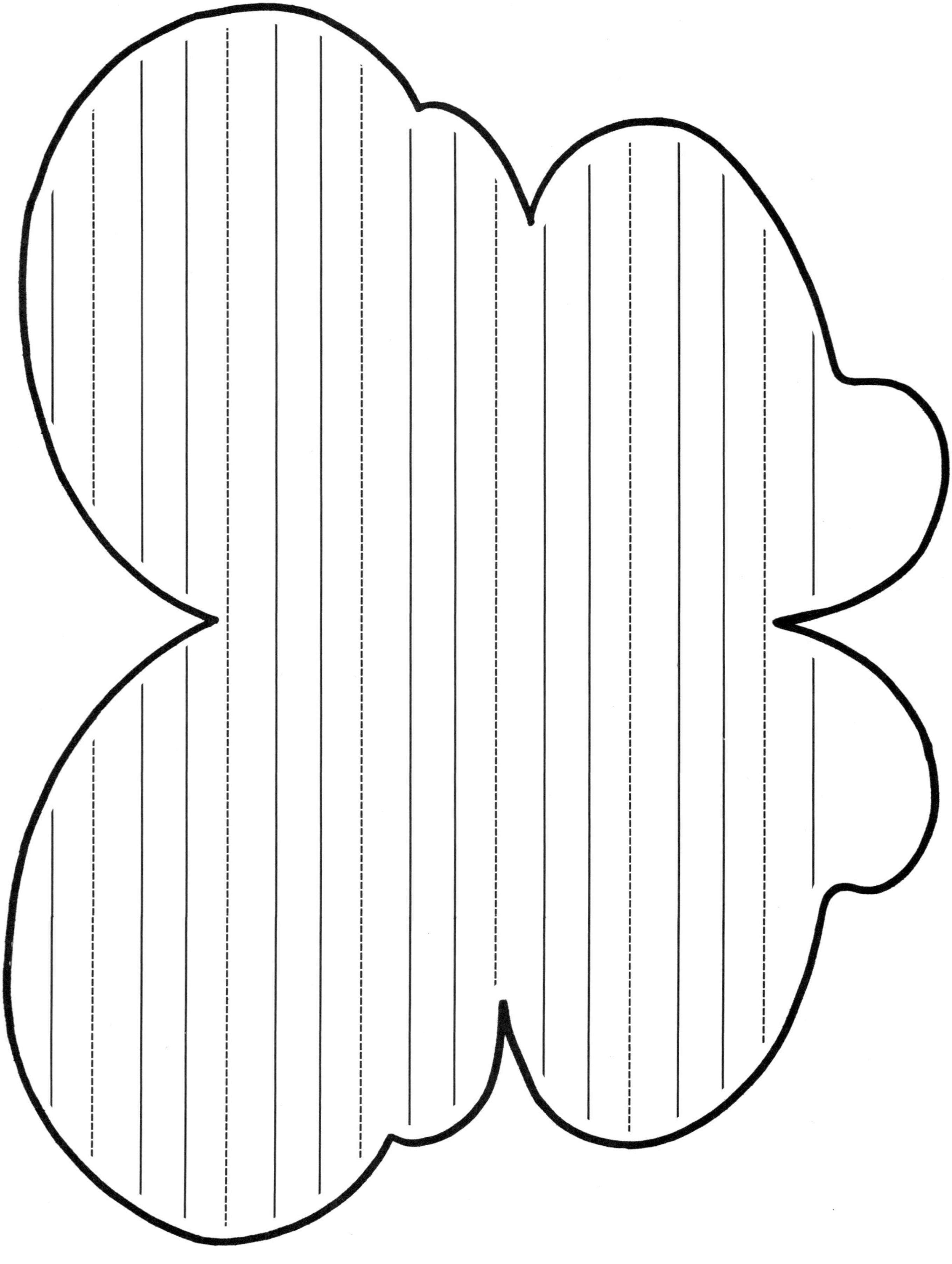

Dino-stories

Story Starters

1. Almost anything about dinosaurs is fascinating to students. Prints and books on this subject are easy to find. Topics for discussion could include how scientists think dinosaurs lived—the climate, the regions where they lived, and their habits.
2. To stimulate students' imaginations, ask them each to picture finding a giant blue egg in the backyard or playground. Tell them to pretend to carry the egg home, wrap it in a blanket, and keep it under the bed. Ask them to write about what happens when the egg hatches, a cute little dinosaur-like creature pops out, and Mom says, "What's that noise?"
3. These story-starter phrases may be printed on the writing sheet master before duplicating, or they may be dictated to the students.

   My pet is a dinosaur . . . Once, a big lizard . . .

   I found a little . . . A dinosaur said . . .

Vocabulary Development

dinosaur	fossil	tyrannosaurus	million
brontosaurus	stegosaurus	swamp	pterodactyl

Additional Activity: Science

Students may use the dinosaur booklets to record facts about dinosaurs. They may want to add drawings or cut-out pictures for illustration.

Bulletin Board Ideas

Cover the board with blue paper. Make tall grass from green construction paper. Pin the completed dinosaur booklets in the grassy areas. On clouds made from white construction paper, print vocabulary words or the names of dinosaurs. Prepare a caption and pin it to the board.

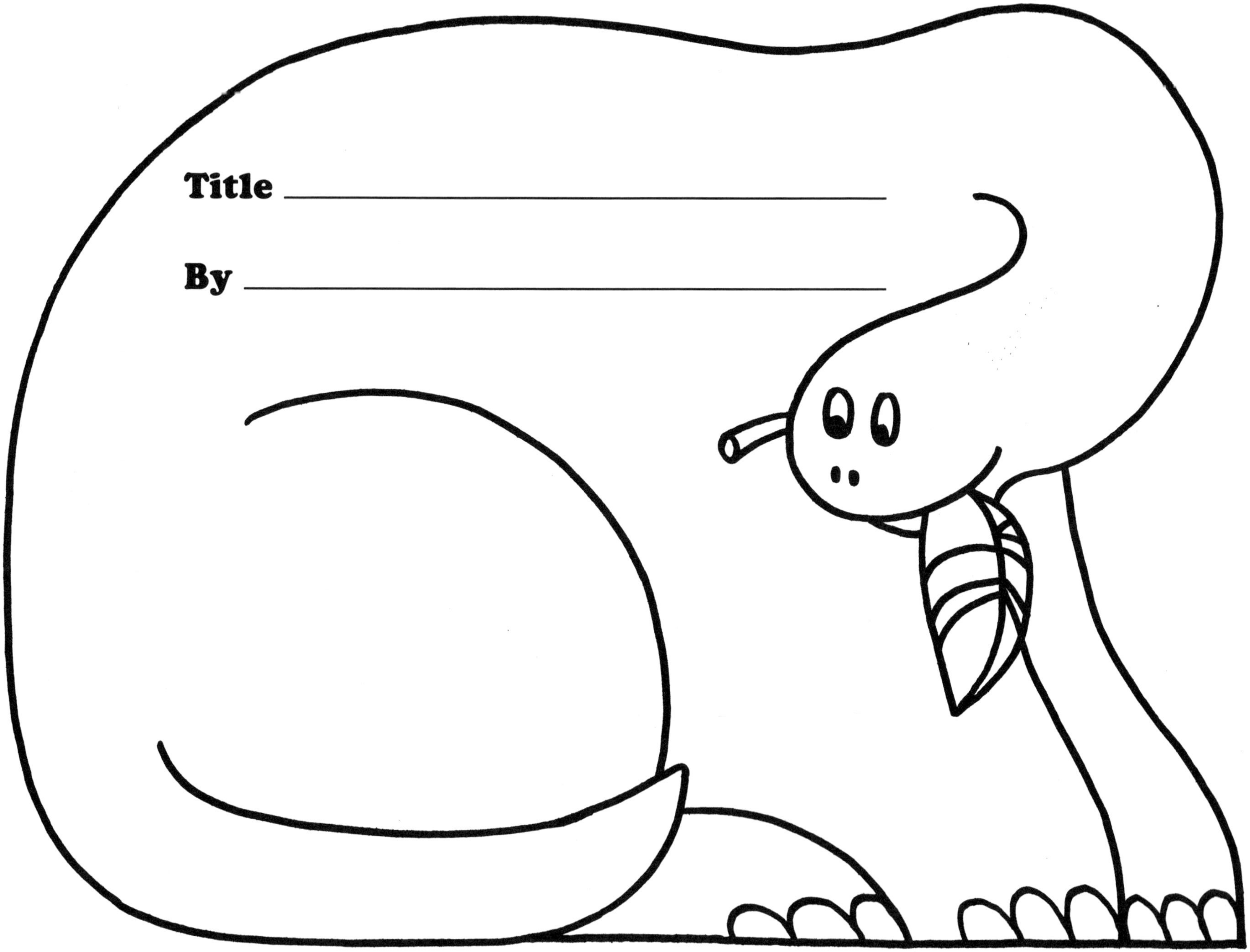
Title
By

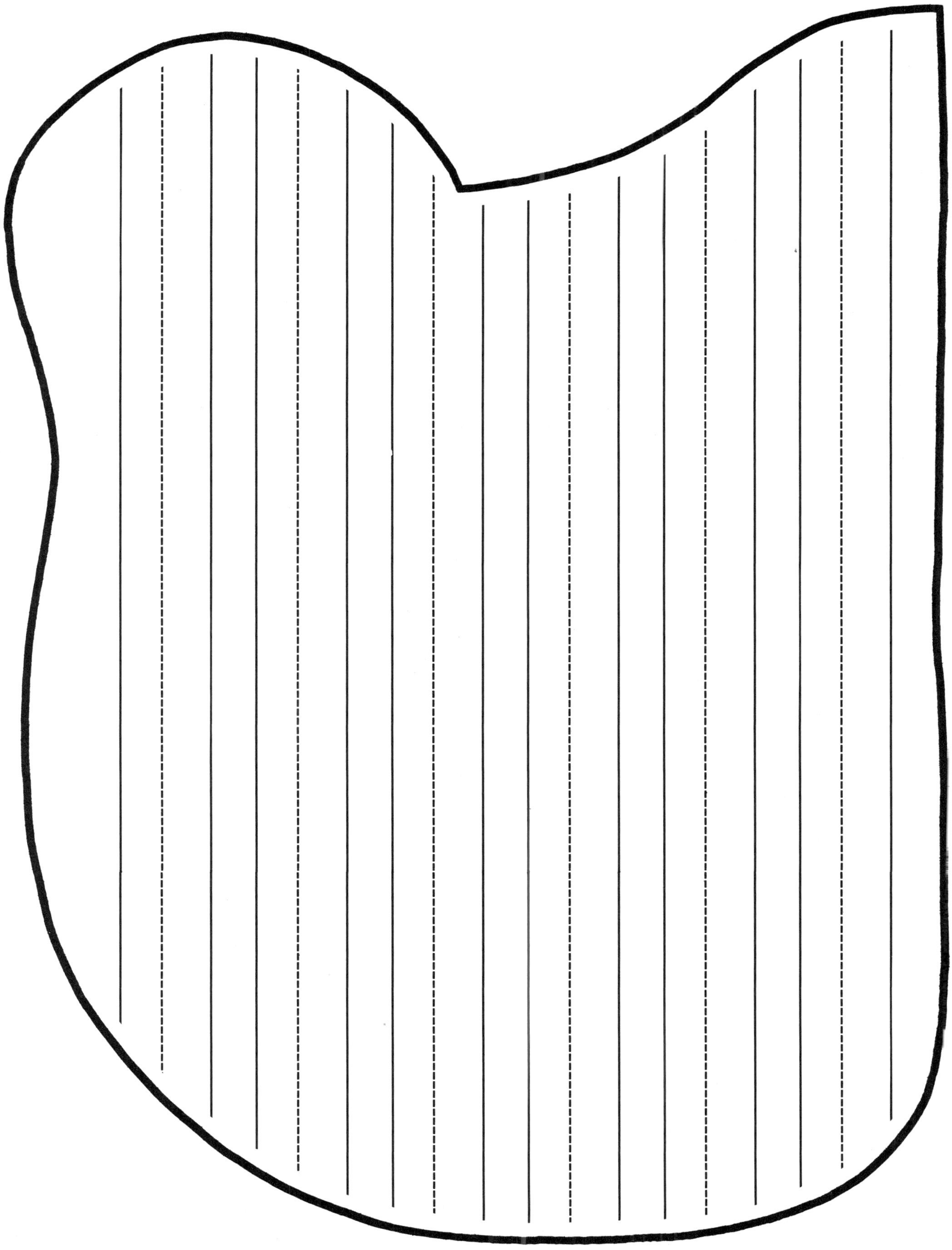

Bunny Tales

Story Starters

1. You may wish to read a story to the students such as *The Tale of Peter Rabbit* or an abbreviated version of *Alice's Adventures in Wonderland.* Topics for discussion could include where rabbits or bunnies live (in nests or burrows), their habits, and what they like to eat.
2. To stimulate imaginations, ask each student to picture a white rabbit hopping onto the playground and whispering, "I've found a magic hat with your name on it, and . . ." Tell the students to write about what happens next.
3. These story-starter phrases may be printed on the writing sheet master before duplicating, or they may be dictated to the students.

   I pulled a rabbit from . . . The little bunny hopped . . .

   The rabbit in our room . . . Once, I fed a bunny some . . .

Vocabulary Development

bunny	cottontail	hopped	magic
rabbit	nest	thumper	carrot

Additional Activity: Science

Arrange to have a domestic rabbit and a cage in your class for a few days. Have the students observe the rabbit's habits and record information in their booklets. Display the students' work.

Bulletin Board Ideas

Cover a bulletin board with blue paper and pin completed bunny booklets on the board. Cut leaves and blossoms from construction paper to create a spring scene. Prepare a caption and pin it to the board.

Title ______________________
By ________________________

Shirt Tales

Story Starters

1. This project may be an "all about me" activity. Ask the students to wear a favorite T-shirt to school. Talk about the messages the shirts have printed on them, and let the students share events that are associated with the purchase of the shirts, such as trips to parks, particular musical groups, or vacations.
2. To stimulate imaginations, ask the students to picture a magic shirt that will, when worn, take each student away to a chosen destination. Tell them that one day, however, the magic shirt takes each of them away to the zoo and lands each one in an animal's cage. Ask each student to write about which animal's cage he or she has landed in, and what happens when the animal sees a visitor in the cage.
3. These story-starter phrases may be printed on the writing sheet master before duplicating, or they may be dictated to the students.

   My favorite . . . My pet's name is . . .

   I want to go to . . . I live with . . .

Vocabulary Development

vacation	magic	family	afraid
trip	zoo	airplane	cage

Additional Activity: Art

Provide crayons or colored marking pens and let students decorate the covers of the shirt booklets with pictures and messages. They may also enjoy doing self-portraits for an "all about me" theme.

Bulletin Board Ideas

Cover the bulletin board with background paper and attach two construction paper tubes. Pin several rows of yarn between the tubes to represent clotheslines. Pin the completed shirt booklets on the clotheslines. Add clouds, grass, and flowers if desired. Prepare a caption and pin it to the board. Hang T-shirts from the clotheslines with miniature plastic clothespins. Write new vocabulary words on the clouds.

Title ______________________
By ______________________

Funny Phone Calls

Story Starters

1. If possible, bring a tape player to class along with some recorded messages designed for telephone answering machines. Play the messages for the students and discuss how the messages are alike and different. Try to record interesting messages—one could be humorous, one a little song, one very straightforward.
2. To stimulate imaginations ask each student to pretend to have a telephone answering device and to compose a message that will tell the caller something about his or her personality, hobbies, or interests. Ask each student to write the message beginning with, "Hello, this is . . ."
3. These story-starter phrases may be printed on the writing sheet master before duplicating, or they may be dictated to the students.

   I answered the telephone, but . . .　　I am calling . . .

   The phone rang and . . .　　Hello, who's there . . .

Vocabulary Development

telephone	number	recording	beep
answer	machine	operator	message

Additional Activity: Language Arts

Set up a listening center with a tape player that has several messages. Ask students to listen carefully to each message and answer a prepared list of questions relating to the messages.

Bulletin Board Ideas

Cover the bulletin board with blue paper, and on it pin telephone poles that have been cut from brown wrapping paper. String black yarn between the poles and then pin the completed telephone booklets over the "wires." Prepare a caption and pin it to the board.

1 2 3
4 5 6
7 8 9
* 0 *
Title ____________________
By ____________________